Heirloom Skills
and Country Pastimes

Also by Deborah Krasner

Celtic: Design and Style in Homes of
Scotland, Ireland, and Wales

From Celtic Hearths: Baked Goods from
Scotland, Ireland, and Wales

Kitchens for Cooks:
Planning Your Perfect Kitchen

Deborah Krasner

Heirloom Skills

and Country Pastimes

Traditional Projects for Kitchen, Home, Garden and Family

Watercolors by the Author

VIKING
STUDIO
BOOKS

VIKING STUDIO BOOKS
Published by the Penguin Group
Penguin Books USA Inc., 375 Hudson Street,
New York, New York 10014, U.S.A.
Penguin Books Ltd, 27 Wrights Lane, London W8 5TZ, England
Penguin Books Australia Ltd, Ringwood, Victoria, Australia
Penguin Books Canada Ltd, 10 Alcorn Avenue,
Toronto, Ontario, Canada M4V 3B2
Penguin Books (N.Z.) Ltd, 182–190 Wairau Road,
Auckland 10, New Zealand

Penguin Books Ltd, Registered Offices:
Harmondsworth, Middlesex, England

First published in 1995 by Viking Penguin,
a division of Penguin Books USA Inc.

1 3 5 7 9 10 8 6 4 2

LIBRARY OF CONGRESS CATALOGING IN PUBLICATION DATA
Krasner, Deborah.
Heirloom skills and country pastimes: traditional projects for kitchen,
home, and garden/Deborah Krasner; paintings by the author.
p. cm.
ISBN 0-670-85168-X
1. Handicraft. 2. Nature craft. 3. Herbs—Utilization.
4. Gardening. I. Title.
TT157.K65   1995
670—dc20   94-5427

Printed in Singapore
Set in Heirloom

For Margaret, William, and Katie Tabb,
who do so much to make our
country life possible

Contents

Useful Arts

Play

Sources

Introduction

Heirloom skills are the ways our forebears made their lives more pleasant. In the not-so-distant past, sweet-scented cleansers, cosmetics, shampoos, and soaps were made at home; one-of-a-kind garments were knitted and sewn without benefit of printed patterns, and garden plots provided ingredients for food, beauty preparations, and medicines.

Country pastimes are the things we do today to carry on that independent spirit of making things at home, using wit and skill to enrich our lives and surroundings.

As you will see, this isn't a book about making cunning bird feeders out of old bleach bottles—it isn't about the delights of crafting. Rather, it is a kind of personal illustrated journal of my family's and my discovery of the joys of country living, which have grown as our Vermont roots deepen and as our children teach us the special value of time at home together.

My husband and I and our two daughters have been living in rural Vermont for seven years. Because I am the daughter and granddaughter of enthusiastic gardeners, I spent most of my childhood trying to avoid digging and weeding assignments. Laboring unwillingly in the hot sun,

I resolved never to have a garden of my own when I grew up.

In fact, we became possessed by our first modest flower garden six years ago, but only after our friend Andrea Darrow was dismayed that we could put so much energy into our house and yet leave the landscape so un-kempt. One day when she was visiting, she began to heave boulders around and do mysterious things with shovels. At the end of an afternoon of her Amazonian efforts, we were the owners of a series of three small, level terraces inhabited by transplanted pieces of her own perennial garden (which had, in turn, been planted with divisions from her grandmother's garden). Looking at that tiny garden carved out of the brush beyond our kitchen windows weakened my defiant childhood resolution—and after only a few days of protecting those infant transplants, I found myself smitten with gardening.

Bulbs about to burst into bloom

Andrea's old-fashioned perennials led me to an obsession with antique sweet-scented roses, for which we built the stone wall planting terraces and sapling arch, inter-planting them with blue and purple delphiniums and white fox-gloves. Then we expanded the entire garden area by rerouting the dirt road that had run in front of our house to a more distant spot, and by leveling and building up what had been road into garden spaces. These we have filled, thanks to the advice and generosity of every gardener we know, with a rich blend of blooming trees, bushes, and plants: monardas, more roses, lupines, poppies, two magnolia trees, weeping crab apples, peonies, and tulip bulbs for a spring display. Dutch landscaper Edwin de Bruijn built us round patios of antique brick and created the planting beds that encircle them. His suggestion that patio edges could be softened with containers started us on outdoor potted plants.

Once we had the flowers well under way, we returned to the old vegetable garden in the field below the house, trying to make it beautiful in its own right. We built raised beds in classic French <u>potager</u> forms, and last year extended its boundaries with berry bushes, asparagus, rhubarb, and the beginnings of an orchard. We connected the lower food gardens and the upper flower gardens via a wildflower meadow.

As I look back on it now, the project seems much more cohesive than it actually was. We bumbled along chaotically, falling in love with plants or species and shoving them in wherever there was any planting space. As we put more thought and energy into the garden, our children began to plant and till alongside us. In the interest of generating future gardeners, we try never to make our daughters work against their will.

Gardening led inevitably to ecology, as plants needed fertilizer and water, and produced a profusion of herbs and flowers we wanted somehow to use. Building the compost area was one of our earliest (and simplest) projects, and had the added benefit of making it easier to be relaxed about uneaten food on the children's plates. Becoming aware of the connection between kitchen and garden meant not only that food went back into food, but also that water could have more than one life. Although we are lucky to have a well that doesn't go dry, we still are glad to get as much use out of our water as possible, using it first for dish-washing and then for plants.

Our home is an 1883 hay barn that we've been renovat-ing for the past seventeen years (it was our summer house before it became our full-time home). We lived in design-conscious Denmark for two years in the 1980s, and returned to Vermont filled with ideas and excitement. When we began renovating, our inspiration was Scandinavian. We have pickled all our floors and trim, and have painted grain on porch rockers and the children's furniture. Further inspired by Scandinavian methods for cheering ourselves through dark winters, we keep candles flickering and scented bulbs growing all over the house, and have taught the children how to knit their own sweaters and make simple skirts.

Summer brings us back out-of-doors to plant play houses along with gardens and to watch the children sail over the flowers on the long arc of a tire swing. Our time from the end of summer into early autumn is filled with harvest rituals of canning and preserving, while our daughters braid onions into kitchen garlands.

Monarda, or bee balm, is fragrant and loved by bees. It also makes a good tea.

Gardening

Starting Seeds

Starting seeds on a sunny windowsill is an exciting and economical way to begin building your garden. Quantities of plants (such as perennials) that would otherwise be unaffordable can be started for pennies, and exotic varieties of flowers and vegetables can make your garden glow.

In climates with short growing seasons, a great many plants need to be started indoors before the ground outside is frost-free. The cost of a packet of seed and planting materials will usually be less than buying a six-pack of young plants that someone else has started, and will yield a far greater number of plants.

For mass plantings I start perennials such as delphiniums, foxgloves, and lavender; hard-to-find annuals like Shungiku edible chrysanthemum, elephant-head amaranth, and heliotrope; and unusual and heirloom varieties of vegetables like ribbed Florentine tomatoes, flageolets, celeriac, and fennel. I also start a variety of peppers, eggplants, onions, melons, and leaf lettuces for early harvesting. (See the Sources section for suppliers of unhybridized and other unusual heirloom seeds, and edible flowers, fruits, and vegetables.)

Seeds can be germinated in egg cartons, milk or yogurt

containers, wooden flats, or commercially made planting containers. Plants do best when they are placed in a warm, sunny spot with few drafts. Grow lights and root heaters are available from garden suppliers, but I find that the east- and south-facing windowsills near my woodstove do just as well.

I use inexpensive (and reusable) three-part plastic planter trays. They consist of a series of cells for planting, an under-tray flat to set the planting cells in, and a clear plastic cover that fits over the whole to create a mini-greenhouse.

Using a soil-based seed-starting medium, I dump a portion of the medium into a large kitchen mixing bowl, add some warm water, and mix it with a long wooden spoon. I want the soil to be well dampened and warm, but not sopping wet. It should compress when I squeeze a small handful, but not drip. When it is the right consistency, I spoon it into each planting cell, pushing it down gently with my finger to make sure there are no large air holes (although little air pockets are good).

I use tweezers to plant two

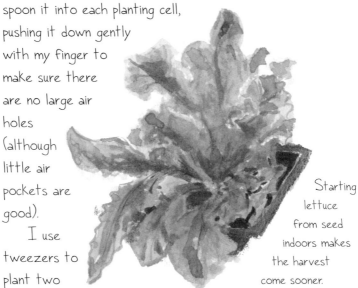

Starting lettuce from seed indoors makes the harvest come sooner.

4

seeds in each pot (I put in a second seed because few packets have 100 percent germination rates; if both seeds do germinate, I thin out the smaller plant). Make sure the soil cover is about three times the depth of the seed (for a $1/8$-inch seed, the cover should be about $3/8$-inch of soil). The great advantage of using a moistened soil medium is that there is no need to top-water the new seeds, which could redistribute them.

Because I plant a number of different seeds in various sections of each mini-greenhouse, I tape the empty packet to the outside of the under-tray flat, or make small paper labels to tape on, noting the date, variety, number, and location of seeds planted. (If the label were inside the cover, it would need to be waterproof.)

Seeds need varying amounts of growing time before transplanting. Onions are sown 12 to 14 weeks before the last frost free date; peppers and eggplants need 8 to 10 weeks; tomatoes grow for 6 to 8 weeks before they need transplanting; and lettuces, brassicas, and melons need between 2 weeks and a month of lead time. New mini-greenhouses are planted every week and older ones are moved to new locations in the house, so that being close to the warm woodstove will help the youngest seeds to germinate. All of the flats are regularly turned in relation to the light, to encourage the plants to grow straight.

Most garden plants germinate in 2 to 3 weeks (the germination time is usually listed on the seed packet or in the garden catalog). I always feel impatient, waiting for the seeds to come up.

It's important not to let the seedlings get too dry or too damp while they are growing. Usually they don't require any extra water until some time after they have sprouted, assuming that the cover is put on tightly. I check the soil every few days, especially if plants are close to a heat source that could dry them out rapidly. If the soil seems dry and the interior of the cover is clear of drops of moisture, I gently mist the surface and replace the top to keep the new moisture in.

As the plants get too tall to fit under the cover, I begin to water them regularly from below by pouring a little water directly into the underflat, which I have lined with a layer of newspapers. There are also commercially made wicking materials designed to line the flat under the planting cells. (The wicking pad absorbs the water and delivers it slowly to the bottom of the seedling container.) It is also possible to water or mist the seedlings gently from above.

Plants that suffer from having their roots disturbed, such as Oriental poppies, melons, or celeriac, can be started in peat plugs, which can later be planted directly in the ground. Plants that need more room to grow, such as tomatoes, broccoli, and peppers, can be planted in larger cells, and then be transplanted into even larger containers before being hardened off. "Hardening off" is the process of bringing plants outside into light shade for gradually longer periods each day, until they are ready to be outdoors all the time and transplanted directly into the earth. This process takes about a week.

Sapling Arch

We made a sapling arch over the stone steps of our garden to mark the path and entrance to the rose garden. We had lots of newly cut green maple saplings, about 1 to 3 inches in diameter, that were a by-product of clearing the hillside of brush.

We gathered a pile of saplings and laid them along the ground, slightly overlapping, like this:

Two of us worked together, winding the soft wood around the next piece, making a sort of twisted rope of young trees. We used green plastic-coated wire (florist's wire) to hold the trees in place, binding them together about every foot or so. Any weather-resistant wire would have done equally well.

If one part of a tree was thick, we paired it with a thinner sapling, overlapping, so that every point was strengthened. When we thought the construction looked long and thick enough, we tried bending it into an arch to see if it was the right length. It is always possible to clip

Rosa
'William Baffin'
grows toward hops
along the sapling arch.

the ends shorter, or to add more saplings to increase the length.

We used a heavy crowbar to bang a thin hole into the earth on each side of the steps, and we sank a length of old steel rebar, left over from a cementing project, into each hole. We left about 8 inches of rebar above the ground.

We put the arch up and pushed the ends into the earth next to the exposed pipe. Then we tied the wood to the pipe, using the metal as an anchor. We added some rock to the arch base for further support.

Our arch is four years old, about 14 feet high, and has survived many high winds, blizzards, and showers. Hops twine up it, and climbing nasturtiums. Last year, in addition to the perennial (and somewhat invasive) hops, which we left on one side of the arch, we planted a hardy climbing rose—'William Baffin,' an extremely vigorous pink rose that can grow to 8 feet and is disease-resistant. (To find 'William Baffin' and other hardy and/or antique roses, see the Sources section.)

Planting a Container

I started filling terra-cotta containers with flowering plants when our brick patio was first built—it looked raw and bare, and needed softening. My first efforts were planted in ordinary clay flowerpots of different sizes—pots filled with a single variety of pansies, nasturtiums, geraniums, or petunias—which looked just wonderful massed together.

Azure-blue pearl petunias planted in a strawberry pot

Wanting a container with a more vertical note, I filled a tall strawberry pot with miniature azure-blue pearl multi-flora petunias, and I liked that combination so much that it is one I repeat every year. I've since gone on to greater heights with containers, adding vines, like the heirloom "canary vine," that twine around poles or up strings attached to the house, surrounded by more bushy and down-trailing plants. (See Sources for suppliers of seeds for unusual flowers, vines, and trailing plants.)

The delight that containers provide is akin to the pleasure that comes from building dollhouses—you can make a miniature world, a landscape with easily controlled combinations of color and form. But because containers are designed to be seen up close, particular attention to the design, color, and form of plants is essential.

In general, containers work best when the following design ideas are kept in mind.

First, plant the tallest plants in the center, with medium-height plants surrounding them and trailing plants to hide and soften the edges of the pot.

Also, make sure that these plants flower continuously, or plan succession plantings if they don't. For example, a container with ivy as the underplanting might have successive plantings of spring bulbs, followed by all-summer-long flowers like geraniums or petunias. A continuously flowering container could feature a mix of geraniums, verbenas, pinks, dusty miller (which provides a gray foil to enliven the colors of the flowers and foliage), and large striped petunias.

Place plants closely together, so that the container

Malope is an uncommon annual, good for container planting.

Looking into malope's blossom

immediately looks lush and full. Aim for a living tapestry of light with dark, small with large, daintily leaved with heroic-ally statured. Plan colors to complement one another, and keep in mind that a monochromatic container can be anything but monotonous. One of my favorite arrangements uses a matched set of weathered gray whiskey half-barrels that sit on either side of the front door. They are planted each summer with a wide assortment of scented white flowering plants of different heights and habits, including moonflowers, which climb up a string tied to a pole in the middle of each planter and are tied together onto a projecting nail above the center of the front door. This creates a gothic arch that frames the entrance with night-blooming flowers.

A well-drained soil or planting medium is also essential to the success of a container arrangement. Make sure the container itself has adequate drainage holes, and put a layer of gravel on the bottom to aid in good drainage. Elevating containers on bricks aids air circulation, which roots need to prevent rotting.

When reusing old clay pots, scrub them with a mild bleach solution to prevent mold and disease. Be sure to rinse very well with clear water. Alternatively, if you love (as I do) the look of green-tinged age on the outside of an unglazed clay pot, rub it with yogurt or buttermilk to encourage moss to grow.

Plants are stressed by close planting, which forces them to compete for nutrients and moisture, so fertilizing container plants is essential. A soilless mix, spiked with sprinkles of slow-release fertilizer (14-14-14) and supplemented with alternate-week applications of a water-soluble fertilizer (I prefer fish emulsion—available from Gardener's Supply; see Sources), will aid health and encourage prolific flowering.

Regular maintenance is also required—deadhead flowers daily to encourage new blooms, and watch for pests so that you can catch them before they take over. Try to make a habit of testing the soil daily for dryness. I find in very hot weather in a sunny location that it is sometimes necessary to water more than once a day!

Annual flowers well suited to container plantings include pansies (I love the "watercolor" strain), marigolds, dwarf salvias (available in deep "wine and jewel-toned" colors), mignonette, annual phlox, miniature ('Little Sweetheart') sweet peas, carnations, globe amaranths, strawflowers, columbines, pinks, and sweet williams.

Ivy, lobelias, and climbing or trailing nasturtiums are good choices for planting the container's outer edge.

Note that plants that may be hardy in the ground over

winter are considerably less hardy in exposed containers. If you are planting perennials, shrubs, or trees in containers, it makes good sense to replant them in the ground in the fall, or to bring them in for the winter.

Clay containers cannot withstand freezing, and must be protected in cold climates by covering and wrapping empty pots left outside to be sure that no moisture can penetrate the clay, or by bringing them into a dry space for winter.

Plantings need not be limited to flowers—one of my favorite house presents is made by lining a bushel basket with a plastic garbage bag that has had drainage holes punched into it, and a layer of gravel or Styrofoam peanuts added to enhance drainage. I plant it with an edible arrangement of mixed radishes, leaf lettuces, nasturtiums, dwarf sunflowers, and tiny zinnias to make a container planting that is delicious as well as decorative. (See Sources for edible garden seed suppliers.) Remember to fertilize regularly, and enclose a small bottle of organic fertilizer with the gift card so that the recipient can harvest a good crop.

A container filled with edibles— radishes white and radishes red, leaf lettuces, and peppery nasturtiums in a bushel basket

13

Window Boxes

Window boxes filled with bright flowers are one of the easiest ways to add great charm to a building's exterior and give landless apartment dwellers opportunities for gardening pleasure. But window boxes can also provide country houses with another jolt of color and aroma, and are especially lovely on an upper floor where a close experience of growing things is often impossible.

Window boxes can be homemade or purchased, but they must be strongly built and well anchored to the building, using appropriate hardware to support the weight of soil and plants. And because such plantings require attention throughout the seasons, they must be located below an opening window. If your house is like ours and has outward-opening casement windows, be sure to leave room for both the path of the window and the growing plants by setting the window box well below the level of the sill.

Like all other container arrangements, window boxes require vigilant watering and feeding, close planting in a well-drained medium and box, and attention to pests and deadheading.

Unlike freestanding containers, which are designed to be

Deep red nasturtiums, full-face and profile

viewed from all sides, a window box functions as a kind of stage set facing the street. The plants are arranged in descending levels, with the tallest plants at the rear, near the window. In front of these are shorter or sprawling plants, which can be used to compose the center or the foreground, depending on the depth of the window box and the forms of the plants. Sometimes window boxes look best with three different rows and heights of plants, particularly when the foreground row trails over the front edge of the box.

A homey cottage garden planting in a sunny window box can be made by crowding in a mixture of medium to tall rudbeckia (black-eyed Susans) and dwarf moss roses with shorter front plantings of dwarf salvia and sweet alyssum. Trailing blue lobelia can soften the front edge of a not-too-sunny box.

My favorite window box uses hanging flowering vines

to create a cooling screen of flowers suspended over the downstairs window. Long, trailing nasturtiums are best used for this purpose, and can create a traffic-stopping effect. Boston's Isabella Stewart Gardner Museum has such second-story window boxes on display, a witty reference to a Monet painting that depicts the same image. Other great trailing possibilities include morning glories in pinks or blues, or night-scented and night-blooming white moonflowers. Such plantings allow both insiders and outsiders to revel in waterfalls of bloom.

Like other containers, window boxes can also look splendid when filled with a single species, and are particularly well suited to seasonal arrangements. For spring bloom, bury bulbs in the fall. Plant tulips deepest, and interplant them with hyacinths or narcissus for the earliest display. Each of these bulbs will flower in its time, and when they are all spent, dig them out and replant the container with small white marguerites for midsummer pleasure. As the daisies fade, remove them and replant the box with a single row of fall-blooming purple cabbages, which get even more attractive as they go to seed.

After these fade, dig out their roots, mix some compost and manure into the soil, sprinkle with bulb booster, and plant next spring's bulbs to keep the cycle going. Winter window boxes can be "mulched" with evergreen cuttings arranged on the surface of the soil to provide attractive cover until spring.

For the Earth

Composting

As my children say, compost is <u>good</u> garbage. It's good in visible ways as a gratifying recycling method; it also carries a psychological benefit. Having a compost pile has allowed us to abandon the dubious virtues of the "clean-plate club."

Composting is a kind of alchemy—the heat of a pile transforms garbage into fertile soil. Compost piles are made of plant materials, such as grass clippings and autumn leaves; kitchen food wastes, usually excluding meat, poultry, and fish because they can attract animals; and unbleached paper, such as coffee filters, tea bags, and paper towels. Composted soil immediately improves the health of anything planted in or under it. (When compost is placed around growing plants, or lightly scratched into the surrounding soil, it is called topdressing.) Creating your own compost pile is the single best thing you can do for all of your plants, as well as for your local landfill.

There are many ways to make a compost area, although the principle behind all compost piles is essentially the same: alternating layers of wet (often called green, because they are fresh) and dry (often called brown)

A two-bin container allows you to make fresh compost while an earlier pile ages.

materials are contained in a compact area so that rotting can occur efficiently. Dried materials, such as hay or fallen leaves, are high in carbon; wet materials, like kitchen waste, are high in nitrogen. The ideal compost mix is higher in carbon than in nitrogen, although in practice it seems to make little difference as long as the pile holds a good variety of materials. Adding some rich garden soil is a good idea to encourage the growth of soil microorganisms, and manure is always a fine addition to any compost pile. Gardener and author Dick Raymond suggests adding alfalfa meal, which he has found to be the best "good bacteria" activator, to the pile. It's a useful and easily implemented suggestion, because alfalfa meal is readily available in the form of Litter Green cat litter (don't let your cat use it first, or you'll risk catching toxoplasmosis) and rabbit food pellets enriched with alfalfa, as well as in bags of horse feed. Sprinkle on a layer of alfalfa meal after each layer of organic material (kitchen waste or garden debris) is added. Other good compost activators are aged manure, bonemeal, wood ashes, and peat moss (unfortunately, a nonrenewable resource).

You can purchase compost bins and compost tumblers (see

Sources), which make it unnecessary to turn the pile, and produce compost most rapidly, or you can build a bin yourself. All compost bins are constructed with ventilated walls, so that air can reach the interior of the pile. Bins can be made by dry-laying courses of cement blocks (on their sides, holes facing outward) to form a square; by nailing four wooden pallets into posts anchored in the ground; or by laying railroad ties "log cabin-style" to create a ventilated square.

The simplest compost bin or cage can be constructed with concrete-reinforcing wire mesh and a few extra strands of wire to hold it together. Here's how:

Cut a piece of mesh 3 feet high and 9 feet long; it will start to roll immediately into a circle. Fasten the edges together with wire to make the bin rigid. Set it on an unobtrusive piece of level ground where it will be convenient to kitchen and garden

To make the foundation of the pile, lay a coarse layer of organic material (for drainage), such as cornstalks, small branches, or hay. Sprinkle in a handful of alfalfa meal or bonemeal (available from garden centers) or any other "good bacteria" source from the list above to activate the pile. Add in layers of kitchen waste, and your choice (mix and match as available) of manure, more alfalfa meal or bonemeal, wood ashes, peat moss, grass clippings, and/or shredded leaves, alternating these relatively fine materials with coarser stuff such as stalks, hay, and branches. Try to alternate layers of wet and dry materials.

In practice, it is a simple matter to throw in a bucket of kitchen waste every few days, spread it into a thin layer with a rake or pitchfork, sprinkle it with manure, wood ashes, or alfalfa meal, and put a layer of hay on top. We keep several bales of spoiled hay next to our compost site for this purpose, as well as a small hill of manure from a neighbor's horses. If we lived in more suburban surroundings, a discreet garbage can or two filled with wood ashes and alfalfa meal or a large bag of peat moss would serve a similar function. If we still lived in a city, I'd buy a small compost tumbler, so that the process would be as quick and efficient as possible.

Compost piles need moisture. When first constructing a pile, it makes sense to wet it down, but we find that rain and snow usually keep our pile at a good level of moisture. Obviously, dry climates will require that you attend to the moisture needs of a compost pile, and a continually humid climate will require a compost bin roof made of a breathable material like canvas, burlap, or wood.

Remember to keep the center of the pile loose to allow air to circulate; the outer edges can be compacted to ensure contact between the layers of the pile. The pile can be aerated with a crowbar or an aerating tool, and you can check the internal temperature with a thermometer (a "cooking" compost pile will heat up to 140 to 150 degrees before cooling down). When the pile stops heating, the compost process should be complete. You'll know it even without a thermometer, because you'll see lots of good crumbly black earth at the bottom of the pile. If the pile seems incompletely composted, it can be "stirred" by forking the material at the edges to the center, and remoistening if necessary.

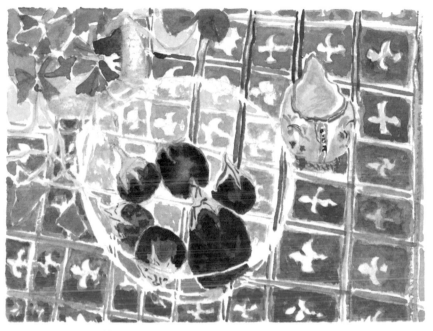

These miniature Japanese eggplants grow well
in compost-enriched soil.

The entire pile can be turned in this way: remove the wire mesh and reposition it on a neighboring bit of ground. Then fork the whole mass into the empty bin, so that the old "top of the pile" becomes the new "bottom of the pile."

All of this moving and aerating substantially reduces the amount of time needed—often as little as 4 to 5 weeks—to produce usable compost. However, many lazy gardeners (myself among them) simply fill up a bin layer by layer, sprinkling dry materials over every layer of wet kitchen waste. When one bin is full, we start a new one next door to it, occasionally adding a bit of finished compost from the bottom of the oldest bin to jump-start the growth of good bacteria and microorganisms in the new bin.

This lazy method is a much lengthier process, stretching over three summers. We usually have three bins working simultaneously: one is new, one is aging, and one is finished (or nearly finished).

Compost piles do not (should not) smell bad—if there is any odor, it is a sign that the pile needs more air. If your compost pile smells bad, remove as much material as possible and remake the pile on top of a layer of cut branches (pruning waste) or anything else that will not pack down readily. As material is added back into the compost, spread dry material generously between layers of wet and poke a stick or a crowbar downward through the pile to create air passages.

Wildflower Meadow

The most satisfying part of last summer's garden was our wildflower meadow. It was filled with the most gorgeous color all summer long, and kept us provided with endless cut flowers until the first October frost. We were thrilled to find it looked just like the picture in the seed catalog and required no work from us beyond the initial planting.

Late last spring, when we tilled the soil for the vegetable garden, we also tilled about a 600-square-foot swath of steep embankment along the edge of the driveway and down into the meadow. We ordered ¼ pound of pure wildflower meadow seed (without grass seed or vermiculite filler) from a company that makes seed selections for our growing area (we chose a "sunny site" mix). Using a large, empty plastic bucket, we blended the seed with about four times its volume of fine white sand.

Monarda can flourish alongside a wildflower meadow

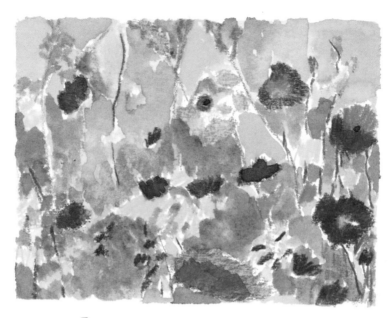

In full bloom, the meadow is filled with color.

We used the sand for two reasons: we wanted to be able to see where we had seeded, and we wanted to disperse the seed to ensure that it wouldn't be planted too closely.

We set down planks of wood to avoid packing the freshly tilled soil (long planks spread the weight of a body out over the whole length of wood, so loose earth is less compacted than it would be from the weight of individual footprints). Standing on the planks, we broadcast seed in fistfuls as evenly as we could, walking along the length of the wood in one direction. Then we moved the planks perpendicular to the original sowing lines and sowed more seed in the same manner. Finally, we spread a layer of loose spoiled hay over the freshly seeded area to prevent the seeds from washing down the steep bank in a heavy rain. Within 4 weeks we had our first blooms!

Our wildflower meadow contained both annual and perennial flowers, but it was the annuals—poppies, cornflowers, Indian paintbrush, baby's breath, black-eyed Susans, and cosmos—that were particularly glorious and abundant. Unfortunately, although those annuals do set seed, they are unlikely to come back in anything like the numbers we had last year. We will see how our meadow looks this year—perhaps more perennials and biennials will be in view—but we are keeping in mind that if we want to maintain the beauty of our original meadow we are going to have to rough up portions of soil and reseed the annuals, or go the whole way and retill and replant every few years.

We were fortunate that the existing weed seeds in the soil didn't germinate in huge numbers. We had some intense sunny, dry weather in the weeks between tilling and seeding, which must have killed some of the dormant weeds. Some wildflower meadow growers advise applying a weed-killer sometime before planting seeds, so that the flowers don't have to compete so much for space. Others advocate a two-season approach to creating a meadow: solarizing the ground with a layer of black plastic to burn out the weed seeds the first season, and then planting the wildflowers the next.

Jim Wilson, author of <u>Landscaping with Wildflowers</u> (Boston: Houghton Mifflin Company, 1992), tells of an easy-to-weed method for starting a small wildflower meadow that was invented by Dr. Robert Lyons. Dr. Lyons starts his mix of seed in peat plugs, a few seeds in each plug. When they are ready to transplant, he sets them in the ground in rows at 18-inch intervals and mulches heavily around them with shredded bark. New transplants are watered well (the mulch helps to prevent evaporation) and then watered as necessary in dry weather. The mulch keeps the weeds from germinating, and any that do manage to grow through it are easily distinguished from the seedlings by their irregular placement. Within 3 weeks of planting, the mulch is hardly visible among stands of blooming wildflowers. Six weeks after planting, the mulch is completely invisible, leaving a dense, weed-free mix of wildflowers.

Black-eyed Susan

Gray Water

I started thinking about gray water when I switched my household cleansers from supermarket specials to a concentrated all-purpose liquid soap that can be diluted to different strengths for different tasks. The manufacturer claimed that the soap not only was biodegradable, but actually had fertilizing capabilities. Having by this time developed a positively nurturing attitude toward the garden (its roses in particular), I was eager to try out these benefits. Figuring out how to save cleaning and dishwashing water became a simple lesson in gray-water usage.

"Gray water" is the term for water that is not clean enough for drinking or cooking but still useful for other applications, such as toilet flushing or watering plants. Some new ecologically-conscious buildings have integral gray-water systems, in which water that would ordinarily flush down a drain is recovered and recycled. But gray-water recovery does not have to be limited to integral house systems; just a few simple changes in dishwashing habits, for instance, can provide a ready source of water that is useful more than once.

The first essential change is to switch to a biodegradable liquid soap. Some, like Shaklee's "Basic H," are

Poured from dishwashing tub to watering can to delicate sunflower seedling, water can be used more than once.

actually formulated to be good for plants, while others are merely not harmful. Read labels carefully before you decide on a new brand.

Next, instead of filling up the sink with soapy water and rinsing in running water, fit two portable basins inside your sink and fill one with soapy water and another with clear water for rinsing. If you find with use that the rinse water is getting too soapy, pour it into a large bucket to save it for flushing purposes before refilling the rinse basin. Although the degree of dirt and soap in the rinse water varies with the meal and the number of dishes, I find that while biodegradable soaps lose their foam faster than commercial varieties, they don't lose their cleaning capabilities.

When the dishes are clean, pour the resulting gray water from the rinse basin into a watering can for your houseplants or directly onto your garden.

The soapiest water can be stored in a large bucket and placed next to a toilet. The next time the toilet needs flushing, instead of using gallons of clean water from the tank, try pouring the bucket of suds directly into the toilet bowl instead. It will flush the toilet's contents automatically (no need to press the flush handle). The bowl will fill with a very small amount of water from the tank—much less than is used when you depress the handle.

Homemade Cleansers and Beauty Aids

Because I object to spending a lot of money for fancy packaging if the product is something I can make myself, I started investigating the ingredient labels on the cleansers and cosmetics I bought on a regular basis. I discovered that freshly made cosmetics can be superior to anything you can buy because they are made with ingredients that could spoil if made on a commercial scale.

You can make your own household cleansers from biodegradable materials available from supermarkets and health-food stores. Such homemade cleansers work as well as commercial ones, cost much less, and do not damage your

Lemons contribute fragrance and astringency to cleansers.

health. Some basic recipes are given here, but I urge readers to get a copy of Annie Berthold-Bond's essential book Clean and Green (Woodstock, NY: Ceres Press), which offers a comprehensive list of recipes for cleaning almost everything nontoxically.

Common pantry ingredients are useful for cleaning, too.

All-Purpose Household Cleanser

To 1 quart of warm water, add 1 teaspoon of bio-degradable liquid soap, 1 teaspoon of borax, and the juice of 1 lemon. Mix gently together and pour into a clean spray or squeeze bottle.

Biodegradable soaps are vegetable oil-based. The borax has antiseptic, antifungal, and antibacterial properties; lemon juice also has these properties and provides grease-cutting power and fragrance too.

Drain Cleanser

Pour $1/2$ cup of baking soda down a sluggish drain, followed by an equal amount of white vinegar or lemon juice (to create a volcano-like reaction). Let stand for 15 minutes, then flush 1 quart or more of boiling water. Repeat if necessary.

Toilet Bowl Cleanser

Pour 1 cup of borax into the toilet bowl and let sit overnight. Flush the next morning. If scrubbing is required, mix
more borax ($^1/_2$ cup of borax to 1 gallon of water) and
scrub well with a good stiff brush.

Laundry Detergent

To get clothes really clean, pour $^1/_4$ cup of biodegradable
liquid laundry soap into the washing machine, then add $^1/_4$ cup
each of borax and washing soda (available at grocery
stores—one brand is Arm & Hammer).

Stains profit from spot treatment with a paste of
liquid biodegradable coconut oil—based soap and washing
soda, rubbed in gently.

Rejuvenating Face Masks and Scrubs

> Warning: Always leave delicate tissue around eyes and
> mouth uncovered, and don't use masks or scrubs if they
> cause skin irritation.

Face Mask #1

Mix 1 tablespoon of brewer's yeast with 1 opened capsule
of wheat-germ oil. Make a paste and apply it to the face.
Let it sit for 10 to 15 minutes; then rinse off with tepid
water. This mask is especially suitable for normal and dry
skin.

Face Mask #2

Mix $1/4$ cup of pure organic bentonite clay with 3 table-spoons of apple cider vinegar. Mix into a smooth paste, adding warm water if necessary. Apply to your clean, damp face and let dry for about 10 minutes. Rinse off gently with tepid water. This mask is very helpful for those who have normal to oily skin

Note: Bentonite clay is available at art supply stores, or by mail order under the brand name Aztec Secret, P.O. Box 19735, Las Vegas, NV 89132.

Exfoliating Scrub

Mix $1/2$ cup of old-fashioned rolled oats, $1/2$ cup of white or yellow cornmeal, and 1 tablespoon of pure organic bentonite clay. Add enough warm water to make a thick paste and apply to your dampened face. Rub gently with fingertips to exfoliate and stimulate the skin. Rinse off well with copious amounts of tepid water.

Herbal Facial

Make an infusion of herbs and flowers by pouring about 4 cups of boiling water over about $1/8$ cup of dried materials in a large bowl. Lean over the bowl and cover your head and the bowl with a towel. Breathe deeply and steam your face for 10 to 15 minutes. Some herbs and flowers you might choose include peppermint leaves, rose petals, fennel leaves, rosemary leaves, and lavender flowers. The steam will open your pores, and the aroma will rejuvenate your spirits. Afterward, a cool rinse will leave your skin glowing.

Hair Tonic/Conditioning Rinse

Pour 2 cups of boiling water over $^1/_8$ cup of dried rosemary or chamomile (twice that amount if the herb is fresh). Let the infusion steep until cool, and then strain out the herb. Apply the tea to wet hair after shampooing to condition and shine. Rosemary is especially good for dark hair, and chamomile brings out the shine in light-colored hair. Plain white vinegar is also a time-honored ingredient for shiny hair—rinse with a mixture of half tea, half vinegar, and watch the dazzle.

Rosemary for remembrance

Homemade Dog Shampoo/Nonpesticide Flea Dip

April Frost, dog trainer extraordinaire of Cornish, New Hampshire, swears by this recipe, which, although (unfortunately) nonbio-degradable, allows people to clean and de-flea their dogs without using pesticides.

> 3 ounces Joy or Dawn dishwashing soap (other brands may contain additives that can cause respiratory distress in some dogs)
> 3 ounces glycerin (available at pharmacies and health-food stores)
> $1^1/_2$ ounces white vinegar
> 1 quart water

Mix ingredients in a plastic bottle. This shampoo will keep indefinitely.

If your dog has fleas, April says, lather well and leave the shampoo on the dog for 15 minutes. The lather will smother the fleas and you won't have to expose yourself or your pet to pyrethrins or other pesticides. Rinse with rosemary hair tonic (see recipe, page 36) to give your pet's coat a good shine and to repel any new fleas that might want to move in.

Making a Home

Pickling Wood

My husband and I love the way new wood looks—that pale freshness veined with grain marks is so beautiful—but we are less happy with wood as it ages, yellows, and darkens.

When we lived in Denmark, we discovered the traditional Scandinavian technique of pickling wood to preserve its original lightness and charm. Here's how it works: A diluted pigment (usually white) is rubbed on clean, newly sanded wood, and then rubbed off with a soft rag. The pigment mix is so watery and thin that the grain of the wood shows through.

Applying a white film allows the wood color to stay fresh-looking and lets the grain show through.

Now that the children are old enough to help, we make our own pigment mix by diluting flat latex (water-based) paint (the cheapest paint will do) with enough water to make a mixture that is the consistency of skim milk. We use a rag or a brush to apply the mix to new wood and then wipe off the excess. You can always apply another coat of color, although we think one coat looks least obtrusive. When the paint/pickle is well dried or cured (allow a day or two of dry weather), you can seal it with 2–3 coats of semigloss water-based urethane. You can also leave it unsealed (for wooden walls only—floors need protection).

We have pickled wood in many forms: floors made of oak, yellow pine, and beech; window trim and baseboards of common pine; and pine-paneled walls, picture frames, doors, and beadboard wainscoting. Pickling completely transforms wooden architectural elements into alluring design statements.

Painting Grain

Trompe l'oeil wood painting is the opposite of pickling—instead of preserving and revealing the grain of the wood with a veil of color, you are using paint to create the appearance of exuberant wood grain where it doesn't exist, on top of a solid color surface.

Like pickling, painting wood grain is a traditional Scandinavian technique. In Denmark and Sweden, particularly, wood grain is applied to walls, doors, interior trim, and furniture. In America, painted wood-grain decoration is often seen in Colonial folk art and furniture. Painting grain is great fun to do, although it takes some skill and a good sense of knowing when to stop!

To paint grain on an old four-panel door, first prepare the surfaces: Patch any dents or holes with wood putty and sand all of the surfaces until they are smooth to the touch. (Wear a respirator or dust mask when sanding off old paint—it probably contains lead, and you will want to avoid inhaling it.)

You will need two paint colors: a base color and a grain color. Both paints must match chemically—that is, both must be either oil-based paint or water-based latex paint. Either

43

variety can be used, as each has different advantages and disadvantages:
water-based latex paints are easily
diluted to a glaze with water and dry
quickly, but they wear less well; oil-
based paints have to be diluted with
turpentine, dry slowly, and create fumes as
they dry, but they wear better over time.

I think that natural pigments, also
called "earth colors," give the softest
effect. Reproduction paints, such as
those sold under the brand names
Stubbs Old Village Paints or Old Sturbridge Paints, are made with these
natural pigments (see Sources). When
you are selecting paint, ask your dealer
to point out the earth pigments; from
palest to darkest they are: yellow ocher,
raw sienna, raw umber, burnt ocher, burnt
sienna, and burnt umber.

Decide whether you want a pale
wood effect, like pine or fruitwood

(a pale yellow ocher or raw-sienna base color), or a dark wood effect, like mahogany (a rich red-brown burnt-sienna base color). For "pine," you will also need a container of a deeper color, such as raw umber, to make a glaze for the grain; for "mahogany," you will need burnt umber or a black paint to thin down to a glaze. The glaze color will need to be diluted until it is transparent and about the consistency of skim milk.

You will need two paintbrushes, one to apply the base coat of paint and another, a stiff bristle brush 4 to 6 inches wide, for making the grain marks. A clean rag for rubbing out any errors should be ready at your side.

Paint the whole door with the chosen base color and let it dry completely. You can then start to apply a thinned glazing/graining coat of a deeper color.

When working on a large piece such as a door, paint only one portion at a time with the glaze, so that you can work it easily while it is wet. Starting with one panel, paint on the glaze with the wide bristle brush, leaving the brush marks as visible as possible. Let your hand waver, in

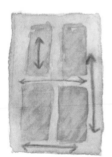

A four-panel door

imitation of wood grain, as you travel down the length of the panel. You can even make a wide curve at the centers of some of the panels to create a knot mark. Paint the grain lines just once down the length of the panel, and let dry. Proceed with each panel in the same way, and then paint the grain in the same way along the raised areas between the panels, moving vertically on the vertical portion and horizontally on the horizontal portion.

When it is dry, your door should look like an old piece with a beautiful wood grain. If you are more ambitious, you can go back over it with a slightly warmer or darker color and a fine brush, applying tiny details to make the whole more convincing. The finished door can be varnished (remember to use a water-base varnish for water-base paint), or it can be waxed with Butcher's Wax and polished.

Forcing Bulbs

Vermont winters seem to last forever, and one way to make them more pleasant is to keep the house filled with flowering and fragrant plants. Paperwhite narcissus and hyacinths are both extremely easy varieties of bulbs to force, and they repay that small effort with a magnificent aroma and lovely form. Amaryllis and tulips are a little more trouble to get going, but are also very rewarding.

I buy paperwhites in boxes of 25 bulbs (I prefer Ziva), as well as tulips, amaryllis, and hyacinths from a wholesale supplier (see Sources), which is the most economical method. Then I have all the flowers I want, plus enough to plant in pretty containers and give as gifts.

Hyacinths and Paperwhites

You can start hyacinths and paperwhites in water, soil, pebbles, or even glass marbles. All work equally well, although bulbs planted in soil seem to last a bit longer. Keep in mind that plants kept cool while growing—i.e., anywhere that stays cooler than 55°F. and doesn't freeze, such as a garage, basement, or mud room—tend to be

Bulbs are containers filled with promise.

shorter and more compact than plants grown in a warm atmosphere. So if you are planning to use paperwhites for a centerpiece, make sure to keep them cool or they'll grow so tall that your dinner companions won't be able to see over them!

Starting Single Bulbs in Water

You will need a container that holds the top of the bulb above water, leaving only the root end touching it. Commercial forcing vases are available, both new and antique. They are sometimes called hyacinth vases, but they work very well for most small bulbs. They're easy to recognize by their distinctive shape.

Many other vases and pots will also be functional mustard pots, for example, and vases with tops that curve inward a third of the way down. Just make sure that the bulb won't fall into the water—it should be supported.

Fill the container with water to the bottom-of-the-bulb level, keeping the bulb point side up. Transfer to a cool, dark place until the bulb starts to grow, about a week. (I use a cold bathroom or a closet.) Check the water and add more whenever the level drops. When the first shoots start coming up, move the plant to a bright but cool windowsill (north is best) to bring on the glorious scent and flower show. I try to keep some bulbs started at all times for continuous flowers all winter.

Starting Multiple Bulbs in Pebbles or Marbles

Starting bulbs in pebbles or marbles is quite easy, too. First put a layer of small stones or marbles in a bowl or shallow pot, and then fit in your bulbs. Pour more stones or marbles around the bulbs to support them in an upright position, and add water to the level of the root end. Now proceed as above, adding fresh water as necessary. Remember—only the roots need water, not the bottom of the bulb, which can rot.

Amaryllis

Amaryllis bulbs are big, exceedingly ugly, and often expensive. They make the effort of growing them worthwhile by producing dramatic, spectacularly colored blossoms year after year. Amaryllis flowers come in many colors, including stripes. It's fun to accumulate a variety of colors over time.

I find the best way to get amaryllis bulbs started is to soak the root end in lukewarm water for about 7 or 8 hours. I do this by putting it in a drinking glass that is wider at the top than the bottom.

After the soaking period, I pot the bulb in a good soil mix that has lots of vermiculite for drainage. I like terra-cotta pots, although plastic pots seem to need watering less frequently. I put a couple of broken potsherds over the drainage hole in the bottom of the pot, then add a layer of gravel and fill the pot partway with soil. Amaryllis bulbs like to have their "shoulders" exposed, so don't plant them

'Star of Holland' amaryllis
is striped red and white.

too deep. Put in the bulb carefully, delicate root side down, and fill the rest of the pot with soil. I water the soil well, and then put the pot on a cool windowsill. I usually see flowers within a month of planting a new bulb.

Occasionally the bulb just sends up leaves, and no flowers. Don't despair; next year, the flowers will amaze you! When only leaves are produced, fertilize the plant with diluted fish emulsion at every other watering, because the bulb needs food to store up energy for next year's flowers.

After the bulb has flowered, leave the stalk to wither at its own rate, and keep the pot watered regularly. The leaves that follow the flower should be fertilized as above, to ensure future blooms.

When summer arrives, take all your amaryllis pots, both old and new, and put them in a shady corner of the garden (or in a dark spot indoors) to go dormant. Don't feed or

water them again until you bring them inside in the fall. Then keep them watered and fertilized until the first green indicates that the cycle is starting again. Hold off on the fertilizer until the flowers have grown, bloomed, and died, and the green leaves alone remain.

Tulips

You have to be sly with tulips, and persuade them that winter has really come and gone in the space of weeks rather than months. Here's how to do it:

I use a thin oval wood mushroom basket that I get from the grocery store (I like the shape). I line it with a small plastic shopping bag and poke a few holes in the bottom of the bag to ensure drainage. After adding a layer of pebbles, I partly fill the basket with soil, tucking in the unsightly edges of the bag I plant the bulbs (4 to 6 fil in a mushroom basket) point side up, flat root side down, and cover them completely with about 4 to 5 inches of soil. Then I water the basket well and set it inside a large dark plastic garbage bag. I tie the end off loosely and cut a few slits in the side of the bag for air.

I put the whole assemblage in a cool place for about a month. The bulbs must be kept from freezing, but only just—a 40-degree temperature is just about ideal. We have a room in the house that we don't keep heated in winter that works well for forcing bulbs, but an unheated (but not freezing) basement or garage (or even a refrigerator) will work for the purpose.

I stick a finger into the soil occasionally to make sure it hasn't dried out. After 8 to 10 weeks, when the bulbs have sent pale shoots above the surface of the soil, it's time to declare spring to the tulips! I bring them into the living room, keep them well watered, and wait for the blossoms. After they've bloomed, I throw away the bulbs, and then I start fresh again the following year.

Useful Arts

Knitting a Sweater Without a Pattern

My daughter Abby learned to knit when she was ten years old by saying a mnemonic rhyme to herself as she stitched: "In through the front door, out through the back, slip around the corner, and off jumps Jack!" By the time she had knit enough to know the stitch by heart, she was ready to learn to purl ("In through the back door, out through the front, tie a ring around it, and off Pearl jumps!"). She was thrilled to have mastered basic knitting, and immediately wanted to make herself a striped sweater.

Not wanting to waste a minute, we assembled odd balls of bulky yarn in vegetable-dyed colors she liked, and a pair of large (size 10) wooden knitting needles.* She didn't have the patience to follow a printed pattern, and we didn't need one anyway, because she wanted to make a simply shaped sweater.

The first step was to find out how many stitches were in an inch of her knitting. She cast on 20 stitches, and began

*Natural dyestuffs and plant-dyed wool are available from Textile Reproductions (see Sources).

Four rectangles
form a
sweater.

to knit, alternating rows of knit and purl. By the time her knitting sample had formed a square, we were able to count her stitch-per-inch gauge. With size 10 needles (wooden needles are less slippery than metal or plastic) and a two-ply worsted wool, Abby's gauge was 3 stitches to the inch.

Next, we measured a favorite sweater to find the right width and length. Abby wanted her handknit sweater to fit her for years to come, so she decided to make it very big and long. Her sweater body front or back measured 18 inches wide and 24 inches long. To figure out how many stitches she needed to cast on, she multiplied 18 inches (the width she wanted) by 3 stitches per inch, to cast on 54 stitches for the back or the front.

Her sweater is constructed of four rectangles—two equal-sized 18- by 24-inch rectangles for the front and back, stitched together along the shoulders with a central opening to create a boat neck, and two for the sleeves. The bottom 2 inches of each front and back panel are ribbed in a knit 1, purl 1 pattern. Each sleeve is made of one rectangle measuring 14 inches wide by 16 inches long, the bottom 2 inches of which are ribbed for cuffs.

Abby started knitting in one color, but after a few inches she decided to make a change. At the start of a purl row she tied a new color securely to the cut thread of the old color and continued knitting, changing colors whenever she felt the design could use a variation. The result was a pattern of irregular stripes across the front of her sweater. Rather than duplicate all of those stripes exactly on the back, she chose not to have the stripes match perfectly at the sides, and just kept on changing colors whenever she felt like it. She could, however, have duplicated the stripes exactly by counting the rows and changing colors on the back just as she had on the front, or she could have made the back a solid color.

Similar choices had to be made for the sleeves—that is, whether the stripe pattern on each sleeve should be

Abby's first sweater is made of stripes using lots of colors.

the same or differently striped, or be a solid color.

When all of the four rectangles were complete and bound off the knitting needles, it was time to sew the sweater together, using a large-eye yarn needle and some scrap yarn. First the front and back were sewn together at the shoulders (right sides together, so that the seam was on the inside), matching the side edges, and leaving the center 6 inches unsewn for the neck opening. Then the sleeve rectangles were centered on each side of the open front and back wrong side up, with the ribbed cuff ends facing outward. Each sleeve was sewn to the body of the sweater in turn, with the seams on the inside. Finally, all that remained was to sew up the "L"-shaped side seams of the arms and the body, and fold down and stitch the selvage at the neck front and back.

Abby's sweater is beautiful, and she will probably be wearing it well into adulthood. Now Lizzie, who is seven years old, is starting to knit, too. Pretty soon she'll be making her own sweater without a pattern, and it will be as unique as her sister's.

Sewing a Simple Skirt

Abby and Lizzie think it is wonderful to be able to make a new twirly elastic-waist skirt in about 20 minutes on a sewing machine. I started sewing them these easy skirts when they were each about three or four years old, and now that the children are older they can sew skirts for themselves. It is very easy to do, and you don't need to buy a pattern! Here's how to do it:

Measure the distance from your waist to the desired length of the skirt. Double this amount, and add another 6 inches for hem and seam allowances. This figure is the amount of fabric you will need to make your skirt, no matter if the fabric is 36 inches or 45 inches wide. (Wider fabric just makes for more gathers at the top.)

You will also need a length of $1/2$- to 1-inch wide elastic, longer by a few inches than your waist measurement, and a safety pin to use in pulling the elastic through

Side seams and an elastic waist quickly transform a length of cotton into a twirly skirt.

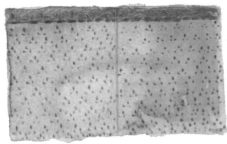

Two rectangles
make a skirt

Thread the elastic
through the waistband tunnel

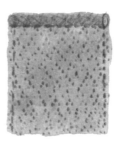

the tunnel you will make on the top edge. If you wish to trim the bottom hem with lace or hem binding, you will need a package of that as well.

Fold the fabric in half along the width, right side to right side. Cut the material on this fold, creating two rectangles.

Match the rectangles together, right side to right side, making sure that any pattern or nap in your fabric runs in the same direction, from top to bottom. Pin the sides to hold them in place, and sew them up using a $1/2$-inch seam allowance. Press the seams open.

To create a tunnel for the elastic waist, first fold over $1/4$ inch of the fabric at the top, iron that down, and fold over again, making sure that your fold is big enough to accommodate the elastic for the waistband and the head of a safety pin. Sew the edge down, leaving a 1-inch gap at one side seam for inserting the elastic.

Measure your waist, sizing the elastic so that it is comfortable rather than tight, and cut it about 2 inches longer than that measurement to allow for overlap.

Pin the safety pin to one end of the elastic and snake it through the tunnel until you come back to where you started. Pull the ends of the elastic free of the fabric, pinning them together to form an unbroken circle through the skirt, allowing a 2-inch overlap. Sew the two ends of the elastic together, making sure the join is strong. Pull the skirt fabric back over the elastic overlap, and blind-stitch the fabric opening by hand.

Try on the skirt and mark the hem. Turn under the first $1/4$ inch and iron it in place (or sew on hem tape or lace edging) and fold again to the desired length. Sew the hem by machine if it has a hemstitch setting, or by hand.

Molded Beeswax Candles

We like to have special candlelit dinners _en famille_ on weekends, and when we use candles we have made ourselves, the event has a special resonance. Candle making is a good winter project: at this time of year dusk comes early, and we appreciate the soft light of candles. Then, too, cool temperatures make it easy to chill molds outdoors.

We use a reproduction tin mold (see Sources for the mold, beeswax, and candlewick cotton). Because wax is very flammable, we melt the wax in a small galvanized bucket (a tall metal can, like a coffee can or olive oil tin, can also be used) set inside a tall stockpot that has been filled to nearly wax-container height with water.

When we are ready to begin, the stockpot is set on the stove with the wax container inside it. (Never put the wax container itself on the heat source.) The heat of the surrounding water melts the wax.

Although pure beeswax candles have a wonderful scent as they burn, they are expensive and tend to burn rapidly because they are so soft. We prefer to melt beeswax and paraffin (available in hardware stores) together—$2/3$ beeswax to $1/3$ paraffin—for added strength, slower burning, and economy.

Before melting the wax (this can be done even days ahead), spray the interior of the candle mold with cooking-oil spray. Invert the mold onto newspaper, and thread through one of the bottom holes a length of candle-wick that is more than twice the length of the candles. Thread the other end of the wick through the next hole, so that a loop is formed on one side, and the two ends are opposite each other. Turn the mold right side up and tie these ends

New tin candle molds look just like antiques.

around a chopstick or twig, making sure that the wicks run tautly up the center of the mold. Repeat for each pair of candles, using a new chopstick for each pair. Using small pieces of children's modeling clay, Play-Doh, or Silly Putty, plug the holes around the bottom of the mold where the wick was threaded. Chill the mold overnight, out-of-doors in a cold climate, or in the freezer.

Keeping wicks uncut allows many pairs of candles to hang from a peg until needed.

Over low heat, melt the wax inside the wax container within the water-filled stockpot. Ensure that all of the wax is completely melted, so that it is hot enough. Using potholders, and working on a surface protected with a layer of newspaper, carefully pour the hot wax into each cavity of the mold, filling it completely. Don't worry if wax overflows the basin or the chopsticks; it is easy to remove with a butter knife when cool.

Let the wax-filled mold cure in a cool place overnight. Cut the top loops of each pair of candles, and, pulling from the chopstick-tied bottoms, ease the candles out of the mold.

Play

Bean Tepees and Sunflower Forts

Gardens create great opportunities to make temporary play-houses out of fast-growing plants. We used to plant beans on poles in the vegetable garden until one day we realized what an enchanting play space a bean tepee could be. Now we make special bean tepees, just for playing in, outside the vegetable garden. If in late spring you plant a bean tepee on one side of the lawn, and a sunflower fort on the other side, your children and their friends can spend their whole summer vacation enjoying these growing "buildings"!

Note: Heirloom unhybridized and unusual bean varieties are available from heirloom seeds listings in the Sources section. Unusual sunflowers can be found in The Cook's Garden, Nichol's, and Shepherd's seed catalogs.

Bean Tepee

To make a bean tepee, collect 6 to 8 branches, 8 feet or more in length, to form the poles, or purchase a commercially available bamboo pole bean-growing kit. If using branches, trim off all protruding limbs and, using a knife or small hatchet, shape the ends into points, so that they are easy to pound into the earth. Select a site with good sun and draw a circle on the ground that is the diameter you wish the tepee to be (about 4 feet is a good size).

Place your poles evenly around the outside of the circle; anchor the bottoms 1 foot deep in the earth and balance the tops of the poles together in the air above the center. (It is useful, but not strictly necessary, to do this with a helper.) Standing on a ladder, if needed, and using twine or plastic-coated wire, firmly tie the tops of the poles together where they cross. Happily, the skeleton will stand through a number of winters, so this work won't need to be repeated next year.

If you want the tepee to be completely enclosed by vines, you can staple chicken wire between all but two of the poles (leaving space for an entrance). Or you can cut two dozen thick 10-to-12-inch-long twigs and set them in the earth at intervals along the perimeter (again leaving a gap between two of the poles). Pound these smaller posts into the ground about 5 or 6 inches deep; they should project upward for about an equal height. Then tie twine from the anchoring twigs to the top center of the poles to provide additional growing supports for your vines.

The tepee skeleton can be covered with a variety of different fast-growing vines. The classic choice is beans, which come in many decorative and delicious varieties. Our favorite is the scarlet runner bean plant, which produces weird long red beans delicious for raw snacking from inside the tepee. You can also plant morning glories, moonflowers,

Creep into the shade of a leafy bean tepee when the sun is high.

climbing nasturtiums, or any combination of vining flowers and beans.

Plant about 5 or 6 seeds at the base of each pole, and more seeds in sets of 2 or 3 along the perimeter of the tepee, following the directions on the seed packet for the best distance between seeds. Water the seeds well (especially if the weather is dry) and stand back and watch them grow! By August the tepee will be full and lush.

Sunflower Fort

To make an August-blooming sunflower fort, start in late spring by marking a rectangle in the ground about 6 feet by 8 feet. Cultivate the earth along those lines, adding fertilizer, manure, or composted earth to enrich it, if necessary, and plant sunflower seeds about 10 to 12 inches apart, leaving a gap of 24 to 36 inches for an entrance—two gaps make a front and a back door (for sneak attacks!).

You can choose a variety of sunflower types, or you can use just one kind. Two especially charming double, or furry, varieties are 'Sole d'Oro' and 'Teddy Bear,' which grow about 5 to 6 feet high. Similar heights are achieved by a wonderful dark red variety called 'Velvet Queen' and a white-flowered variety, 'Italian White.' An even taller, more traditionally colored sunflower is 'Giant Grey Stripe.'

Being smaller than a flower is a remarkable experience! It is also magical to watch the sunflower heads turn through the day toward the sun, facing east in morning and west at night!

' Teddy Bear' sunflower is appropriately fuzzy-looking.

Tire Swings

Five years ago, with substantial help from an experienced tire-swing maker and mountain-climbing friend, Chris O'Brien, we put up a wonderful high-off-the-ground tire swing.

Chris used his climbing sling and pulley to get himself, 50 or 60 feet of strong nylon rope, a cloth pad, and a pruning saw very high in one of our old maple trees. As he pulled himself up, he cut off protruding limbs along the trunk until he found a good outreaching branch that was about 25 feet off the ground. Because of this height the tire swing has a very long path.

He laid the cloth pad (a folded feed bag) over the limb and then unwound the rope until he could find the center. He draped the center of the rope over the padded portion of the limb, and pulled the rest of the rope through the center loop to make a half-hitch knot. He then wound the two lengths of rope around the padded limb a few times for strength.

Coming down to ground level, Chris securely tied the old tire onto the other ends of the rope, again winding the rope around a few times for support before tying additional knots. We drilled some holes in the bottom of the tire so that water would drain out of it when it rains.

The tire swing is one of the most popular play spots in our garden and never seems to lose its appeal. It is so strong that two children can ride it together. Even grown-ups have been known to take a swing.

Chris's help was much appreciated, and dramatic to watch, but now that we know how to make a long tire swing, we can do it ourselves next time with a rented long ladder.

Sailing over the garden

Braiding Onions

One of the best things about growing your own onions is that you can harvest them to make garlands. To do that, the long, leafy tops are left on the onions and are braided onto twine to form long ropes. Braiding is an activity that children enjoy, particularly when their finished plaits are hung as edible decorations.

It's fun to start onions from seed in the early spring and have those same onions draped around the kitchen (and enriching meals) in the fall. Some good sweet Spanish-type onions are 'Ringmaster,' 'Alisa Craig,' and 'Sweet Sandwich' (see Sources for edible garden suppliers).

Onions need light, fertile soil, and should be planted close together (every inch or so) and then thinned to a 4-inch spacing (this spacing also applies to onion sets, if you prefer to start your onions growing from bulbs). Because onions are shallow rooted (the root is what you eat), they need to be mulched in hot weather to keep the soil moist and cool.

Although you can harvest onions almost any time in every stage of their development—from tiny green onion leaves in their infancy (don't take more than one or two per

Onion braids enrich
both decor and cuisine.

plant,
if you
want it to keep
on growing), to
little scallions, to
baby onions—if you have
storage and braiding in mind,
you'll have to wait until the
onion is perfectly ripe and ready. When some or all of the
tops have yellowed and fallen over, knock down the ones
that are still upright with a rake. When all of their tops
are brown, pull up the onions and get ready to braid.

   Braiding onions is a lot like French-braiding hair—each
twist of the braid brings in new material from lower down
the chain. To start, cut a length of twine as long as (or
longer than) you want the garland to be, and lay it flat
along the work surface. Line up your onions over the twine
with the brown leaves facing toward one end, each onion
slightly overlapping the one before. Starting with the first
onion, separate the leaves into three sections, incorporating
the twine into one of the sections, and begin to braid.

When you are about half to three-quarters down the length of the first onion's leaves, begin to incorporate and braid in the next onion, so that the bulb sits on top of the previous braid as the braided rope continues behind it. Continue in this fashion until your garland is as long as you would like it to be.

Cure the braided garland in the sun, or in a well-ventilated dry area, for about 3 to 5 days, until the leaves are brown and dry. One way to do this is to set the braids on top of old window screens supported on sawhorses so that the air can circulate freely around them.

After curing, the braids are ready to be hung for storage, allowing you to cut off onions as needed.

Sources

Heirloom (Old-fashioned, Historic, Unhybridized) and Unusual Flower and Vegetable Seeds for Containers or Gardens

Bounliful Gardens
18001 Shafer Ranch Road
Willits, CA 95490
(707) 459-6410

Old Sturbridge Village
1 Old Sturbridge Village
   Road
Sturbridge, MA 01566
(508) 347-3362

Seeds Blum
Idaho City Stage
Boise, ID 83706
(208) 452-0858

Seeds of Change
1364 Rufina Circle #5
Santa Fe, NM 87501
(505) 438-8080

Thomas Jefferson Center
   for Historic Plants
Monticello
PO Box 316
Charlottesville, VA 22902
(804) 984-9819

Old Roses
   Includes antique and hardy climbing varieties for planting near a sapling arch.

Antique Rose Emporium
Route 5, P.O. Box 143
Brenham, TX 77833
(409) 836-9051

Heirloom Old Garden Roses
24062 Riverside Drive NE
St. Paul, OR 97137
(503) 538-1576

Pickering Nurseries
670 Kingston Road
Pickering, Ontario,
Canada LIV 1A6
(905) 839-2111

Royall River Roses at
   Forevergreen Farm
70 New Gloucester Road
North Yarmouth,
ME 04097
(207) 829-5830

Vintage Gardens
3003 Pleasant Hill Road
Sebastapol, CA 95472
(707) 829-5342

Unusual Flower, Fruit, and
Vegetable Seeds/Container
Plant Materials
   Includes sources for
dwarf and full-sized sunflower
varieties, bean vines, container
flower-seed packages, and
miniature vegetables and edible
flowers for planting a food-
crop container.

   Arbor & Espalier Co.
   4395 Westside Road
   Healdsburg, CA 95448
   (707) 433-6420

   The Cook's Garden
   P.O. Box 535
   Londonderry, VT 05148
   (802) 824-3400

   Edible Landscaping
   P.O. Box 77
   Afton, VA 22920
   (800) 524-4156

Nichol's Garden Nursery
1190 North Pacific Highway
Albany, OR 97321
(503) 928-9280

Shepherd's Garden Seeds
30 Irene Street
Torrington, CT 06790
(203) 482-3638

Bulbs for Indoor Forcing and
for the Garden
   These sources are mostly
for large orders of 25 to 100
bulbs of one variety, including
tulips of every description,
amaryllis (they can be ordered in
sets of three), hyacinths, and
paperwhites.

   McClure & Zimmerman
   108 West Winnebago
   P.O. Box 368
   Friesland, WI 53935
   (414) 326-4220

   Van Engelen Inc.
   313 Maple Street
   Litchfield, CT 06759
   (203) 567-8734

Composting
   Supplies and information for
various methods of composting.

   Gardener's Supply
   128 Intervale Road
   Burlington, VT 05401
   (802) 863-1700

Green Cone (solar
    composter)
P.O. Box 866
Menlo Park, CA 94126
(415) 365-8637

Kemp Compost Tumbler
160 Koser Road
Lititz, PA 17543
(717) 626-5600

Worm-a-Way Composter
10332 Shaver Road
Kalamazoo, MI 49002
(616) 327-0108

Wildflowers for Meadows

Clyde Robin Seed Co.
P.O. Box 2366
Castro Valley, CA 94546

Seeds Trust/High Altiitude
    Gardens
P.O. Box 1048
Hailey, ID 83333
(208) 788-4363

The Vermont Wildflower
    Farm
P.O. Box 5, Route 7
Charlotte, VT 05445

Wildflower Seed Company
P.O. Box 406
St. Helena, CA 95452

Wildseed, Inc.
P.O. Box 308
Eagle Lake, TX 77434

Reproduction and Natural
Pigment Paints

Stubbs Old Village Paints/
    Old Sturbridge Paints
P.O. Box 597
East Allen and Graham
Streets
Allentown, PA 18105

Useful Arts
    Source for beeswax, candle
mold, candlewick cotton, plus
natural dyestuffs like indigo and
cochineal for dyeing your own
yarn.

Textile Reproductions
P.O. Box 48
West Chesterfield,
MA 01084
(413) 296-4437